It began in London's East End in nothing new, a macabre killer was stalking prostitutes, leaving his gruesome calling card etched with a blade in flesh. Regardless of whether Mary Ann "Polly" Nichols was the first of his victims in August or if previous women fell to his knife, Jack the Ripper's infamy became firmly established with the publication of the "Dear Boss" letter in September of that year. In that moment, a horrified fascination for murder began for the public at large.

Since that time, many murderers have plied their bloody trade. Few people remain ignorant of the crimes of BTK Dennis Rader, Ted Bundy, The Green River Killer Gary Ridgeway and Richard Speck. However, for many armchair Sherlocks, more intriguing than these killers -- famous not just for their depravity but for the sheer numbers of murders committed -- are those murderers who got away with it.

Throughout history, many have died at the hands of others, but the most compelling are the crimes never satisfyingly solved due to lack of evidence, unavailable forensic techniques or simply good luck for the offenders. It is those crimes this compilation recounts. While many of the murders that follow will likely remain unsolved, we read them hoping to glean insight and closure. It is a dark path, but you should know you share it with others who feel the same allure.

Chapter 1: Wayne/Burns, Colorado Springs, Colorado

September, 1911

THE DISCOVERY

Mrs. Nettie Ruth stepped out the door of her sister's home just after 9 pm on Sunday, September 17, 1911. She and her sister, Mrs. Alice May Burnham, called "May" by family and friends, had passed a pleasant evening chatting away as the two Burnham children, Nellie (mistakenly listed as "Alice" in contemporary news articles and called "Little May" by family members), aged 6, and John, aged 3, scampered about. By all accounts, May and her husband of 7 years, Arthur John or A.J., got along well despite the fact he was approximately 15 years her senior. As Nettie left her sister's home, May bemoaned that she had a tremendous load of sewing to catch up on. Nettie laughed, noting she had the same struggle, so May suggested Nettie come by the next day so they could work on their stitching chores together. A.J. worked in the kitchen at a nearby sanatorium (Modern Woodman) and typically returned home just one day each week, so May and the children appreciated Nettie's company. Nettie demurred, saying she had other chores to attend to, but asked if she could reschedule for 2:00 Wednesday afternoon, three days away, to which May agreed. It was an appointment that would not be kept.

The next morning, the Burnham's neighbor Mrs. C.L. Brown noticed the blinds were drawn in the tiny Burnham house. Mrs. Brown concluded the family had gone away for some time since the window coverings being pulled was unusual and she saw no sign of May or the children about. A boy from a store knocked at the residence that same morning in an attempt to collect on a bill, but he, too, noted the closed shades. Getting no response at the door, he left, hoping to catch the residents on a different day. He returned Tuesday and Wednesday mornings but noted the house in the same condition.

Wednesday afternoon, Nettie gathered her sewing and set off to her sister's house. She was surprised to find the house closed up and the doors locked. She assumed May had gone to her close friend Anna Merritt's home, just half a block away, so Nettie trundled off to Anna's, perhaps a bit annoyed her sister had forgotten their appointment. When Anna told Nettie she hadn't seen May for several days, fear set in. The women at first silently acknowledged to each other that something was very wrong. Nettie used Anna's phone to call a perplexed A.J. at the sanatorium to see if he knew where his wife might be. He asked if something was wrong, but Nettie had no definitive answers for him at this point. Anna grabbed a key she kept to her good friend's house, and the women hurried down the street. Nettie later said she exclaimed along the way, "Oh, suppose we find May and her babies dead in the house. It would be terrible, terrible!" But the horror would be beyond anything she could imagine.

Anna struggled to unlock the door with her trembling hands. The smell hit them immediately when they finally pushed the door ajar, which opened into the room that functioned as both the kitchen and a bedroom. Nettie noticed the supper dishes from Sunday still upon the table. The bed there appeared not to have been slept in. As they approached the door that separated this multifunctional room from the main bedroom, clutching each other's hands for support, they knew they would find tragedy. But they didn't expect so much blood.

It was difficult to see at first in the darkened room: they could make out only clothing on the bed, shadows throughout the space. As their eyes adjusted, the women first realized that splashes of blood patterned across the walls, such great amounts that the women at first stood rooted, unable to comprehend what they were seeing. Then the figures on the bed became clear—not piles of clothes as they first appeared but instead bodies, one of them clearly a small form the size of little Nellie, her head crushed and bloodied. Screaming with horror, the women ran from the residence to the grocer across the street.

Colorado Springs, Early 1900s

THE SCENE

The authorities converging on the scene found May and John in their beds, beaten to death apparently as they slept, with the covers pulled up to their chins. Nellie's body lay across May's, and the police surmised she had awakened and tried to run from the room. The murderer likely struck late Sunday night or early Monday morning. Autopsy established that May had been pregnant but revealed little other evidence not clear from the scene. All three had crushed skulls and had clearly been pummeled with a heavy object. When A.J. later viewed the bodies, their injuries were so severe that he failed to recognize his own daughter at first.

Aside from the carnage upon the bodies, the house remained largely undisturbed. A bottle of ink by the east window had spilled onto the floor, where clearly someone had tried to wipe up the mess. The murderer apparently slit a window screen to open the latch on the door and then left via the window in order to leave the doors locked, perhaps knocking the ink over in the process. Police found no weapon in the house. A gold watch lay in plain sight, and other jewelry including a diamond ring and pin sat untouched in an easily-accessible drawer, eliminating robbery as a motive for the crime. Police found no footprints from an intruder, and nobody in the area remembered seeing a stranger in the neighborhood, hearing anything untoward or noticing anything else out of the ordinary.

THE REALIZATION

Neighbors thronged to the area as more and more officials appeared on the scene. As word spread about the horrific murders of May and her children, some felt sudden trepidation. The Waynes, friends and neighbors to the Burnhams, also appeared to be out of town. Their house was quiet, shades pulled, and nobody could recall seeing them since Sunday. The nearby grocer Grant Collins had spent time getting to know Henry Wayne just that Sunday afternoon when Wayne and his wife, Blanche, and their infant daughter Blanch, just two years old, spent about 2 ½ hours at the store, chatting with the owner. Business was slow, and Grant enjoyed Henry's company. Watching the bustle about the Burnham house, he realized he not only hadn't seen the Burnhams but neither had he seen the Waynes since that time, an unusually long absence since some member of the two households purchased from the shop nearly every day. The neighbor Mrs. Brown, realizing her earlier assumption that the Burnhams were away, now noted that the Wayne house had been dark and silent the past two days, just like the Burnhams'. Clearly the families were not on a happy outing together.

One neighbor, Mrs. F.E. Campbell, finally voiced the concern so many felt about the Waynes to the authorities combing the Burnham residence. As others chimed in to express concern about the newest family to the area, police rushed to the Waynes' house. Entering through the unlocked back door, they found a similar bloody scene. All three were clearly dead, their heads bashed in. Blanche still sported bracelets on her wrist, but all family members looked as if they had been attacked while asleep, just as with May and John in the horrific scene next door. Cuts and bruises covered the victims' faces and heads. No footprints appeared in the home and none of the house's contents appeared to be disturbed save a screen by the back door that had been cut, seemingly to allow the killer exit from the scene. Detectives surmised a twist of wire found near the back door functioned as a key used to enter the home. While finding more bodies, particularly that of the baby, murdered in the same manner added to neighborhood people's disquiet, a seemingly helpful clue was finally found – a bloody axe by the Waynes' back door.

Blanche Wayne had borrowed the axe from another neighbor, Mrs. J.R. Evans, the previous week. Mrs. Evans had seen the axe at the Waynes' back door earlier in the workweek but assumed the blood on the implement came from chickens until the bodies were discovered. So apparently the murderer had approached the house without a weapon, seizing upon the axe at the Wayne home to butcher the family inside and then attacking the woman and her children next door.

The handle of the axe revealed the most important clue: a fingerprint etched in ink. Fingerprint analysis was a relatively new investigative tool at the time. A U.S. Appeals Court ruled fingerprints admissible for the first time in 1911, the same year as these murders. The New York City Police Department had only been using fingerprints in investigations for five years.

Thursday, the day after finding the grisly scenes, a mill worker named Marshall who had to pass the two homes on his way to and from work, came forward with the information that he had observed a man nearby the houses just after midnight on Sunday. The man's appearance and manner was noteworthy enough that Marshall noted the man's height – approximately the same as A.J. Burnham – and that the cypher wore a "light, soft" hat.

THE SUSPECTS

A.J. Burnham

Suspicion naturally fell upon the sole surviving member of the two families – A.J. Burnham. Police took Burnham into custody early afternoon of the day the bodies were discovered. Someone had called the sanatorium and told Burnham his family was dead, but he didn't learn the details until the deputies picked him up along the road. He had headed home upon hearing the news, hitching a ride for the 12-mile journey in a laundry wagon. His words upon reaching the police were recorded as, "My God! How did it happen? Did they get killed in a railroad accident?"

Besides being the only person in the two families not killed in the attack, Burnham's attitude aroused suspicion. On the remainder of the ride back to the murder scene with the police, he supposedly laughed and joked with the officers. Upon being taken inside, not even the sight of the blood moved him to tears. His cold bearing led many to believe he could be the killer. Although Marshall hadn't yet come forward with his description of the man seen in the wee hours of Monday morning, Burnham wore a light, soft hat.

Burnham had met Henry Wayne when Wayne spent time as a patient in the sanatorium. The two men struck up a friendship. Upon release from the institution, Wayne decided he and his family would like to stay in the area, so Burnham got him a job at the hospital and told Wayne of a house for rent next to his in Colorado Springs. The Waynes had only lived in the house for a few weeks prior to the murders.

Employees at the sanatorium typically received one day off every two weeks, lodging during the work week in a cottage at the institution. Burnham's usual day off was Sunday, but he had requested the previous Wednesday off, instead. His boss, Superintendent Dr. J.A. Rutledge, swore Burnham's movements could be accounted for the entire time. After spending the day peeling hundreds of pounds of potatoes, Burnham knocked off at his usual hour of 7 pm and retired to the cottage he shared with another worker.

Several other men spent time at the cottage that evening, all of whom attested they knew his whereabouts in the cottage until at least 10 pm. The roommate said he heard Burnham several times during the night, as he had a heavy cough due to asthma and tuberculosis, and Burnham appeared at work at his usual early hour the next morning.

Traveling the 12 miles to Colorado Springs from Modern Woodman (pictured at left) in 1911 was no easy feat, either. A healthy man would have difficulty walking that distance and back in the few hours Burnham might have been unaccounted for, and the sanatorium's workers avow Burnham couldn't walk more than several steps without gasping for breath. Dr. Rutledge pointed out that the night watchman at the institution should have heard a car or wagon, and all the Woodman's wagons were accounted for.

Rutledge also said that besides the fact he didn't believe Burnham physically capable of the violence perpetrated in the two households, Burnham and Henry Wayne were fast friends; he saw no animosity between them. Mrs. Ruth felt the marriage a happy one and testified that Burnham doted on his children; he always spent his day off with his little family. She went so far as to telegram Burnham's wealth uncle so the prisoner could get financial support toward his release. Burnham attended his family's funeral under guard, and at the cemetery, May's mother threw her arms around him and wept, declaring her belief in his innocence. Well-known in the Colorado Springs community, nobody came forward with gossip or facts that painted Burnham as a violent, angry or mentally ill man.

From the first, Burnham steadfastly denied any complicity in or knowledge of the crime or who could have committed it. Authorities found small spots of blood on his shirt, which he could not account for. The final determination of Burnham's connection to the murders through these blood spots and the fingerprints have been lost through the decades, but the upshot is that Burnham was released from jail without being charged.

The Ex-Husband

Word circulated in Colorado Springs for a while that a different suspect had not only been arrested for the crime but confessed. The rumor declared May Burnham had a previous husband responsible for killing the two families. While jealousy might account for the ex-husband murdering May and her children, the story didn't put forth a theory as to why the Wayne family was also targeted. In the end, officials declared May Burnham had no ex-husband, and nobody had confessed to the murders.

Tony Donatel

Two days after the discovery of the mutilated bodies, police arrested Tony Donatel, a middle-aged long-time acquaintance of the Burnhams. The arrest apparently stemmed from A.J.'s statements while in custody, alluding to a time he returned home unexpectedly and encountered Donatel with May in a compromising situation. Although Donatel offered an innocent explanation for his presence, Burnham found the situation suspicious enough that he named Donatel as a potential suspect in the attacks. Already working on the theory that jealousy or revenge must be the motive for the murders, Donatel fit into that notion well.

Police found Donatel an interesting suspect for several reasons. For one, Donatel's sanity had been questioned in 1910. Citizens reported seeing him scrubbing the outsides of the various properties he owned, claiming he was eradicating the marks left by witches, who he felt followed him about and harassed him. Although the doctor who examined Donatel at the time refused to institutionalize him, such a history was enough together with Burnham's suggestion to put him in police radar. Clearly, a maniac was responsible for the murders, so any hint of instability was evidence of guilt in their book.

Physically, Donatel matched the sketchy description Marshall had given of his midnight sighting, being about the same height as A.J. Burnham and the owner of a light, soft hat. Donatel's pants contained several spots that looked suspiciously like black ink, and several of his fingers were purportedly black, as well.

Donatel admitted to a "friendly" relationship with Mrs. Burnham but claimed to not even know the family's exact current address, although he did know the general area, which was near his current employment. He told police he was alone in his house Sunday night, where he went after visiting friends, a couple who corroborated that he left their house about 9:30 Sunday night.

Like Burnham, Donatel was never officially charged, released on September 28.

FINAL THOUGHTS

A retired Colorado Springs investigator in the early 21st century began following his hunch that the Burnham/Wayne murderer was a serial killer traveling along the railroad. The tracks ran near the crime scene, and numerous ax murders occurred throughout the country during the period. The scant records and ineffective preservation of some of the evidence hampers his ability to pursue his theory, but it seems as likely a possibility as any, more so than the theory of jealousy or revenge from the lone survivor or a spurned lover that police proposed at the time.

The jealousy/revenge motive simply doesn't wash looking back a century after the deaths. Clearly, the Waynes were murdered first, so if any particular person were the target, it should be one of them unless the killer mistakenly entered the wrong house. The investigation uncovered nobody who seemed to want any of the Waynes dead. So this clever killer was perhaps bumbling enough to attack the wrong family? Even if May Burnham were the focus, however, why would the killer plan his attack and yet not take a weapon with him? Why use the unwieldy ax, demolishing the faces of the victims (including a year-old infant), and then pull the covers up to their shoulders, wash his hands and walk away? It takes a cool customer to bludgeon an entire family in such a frenzy and then calm himself enough to creep unnoticed into the neighbor's house to continue the slaughter. It also seems unlikely the killer could slip back into a normal routine in Colorado Springs without attracting attention, making the transient murderer the most compelling possibility.

Chapter 2: Charles Walton, Lower Quinton, Warwickshire

February, 1945

THE DISCOVERY

On the morning of February 14, 1945, 74-year-old Charles Watson left the home he shared with his 33-year-old niece and adopted daughter, Edith, to work cutting hedges for local farmer Alfred Potter. Though technically retired from his career of training horses, Watson periodically took on farm work when he could to supplement his pension. His savings had dwindled to practically nothing after a large deposit upon his wife's death 15 years earlier from which he had intermittently drawn to get by. Watson took with him two tools – a pitchfork and a slash hook (a small sickle held in one hand) for pruning – and his walking stick and pocket watch but nothing else; Edith noted he left his money at home that morning, as usual.

A man not comfortable socializing, although by no means a social pariah, Watson typically returned home immediately after his workday: 4 o'clock. Therefore, when he wasn't home by 6 o'clock, Edith began to worry, thinking he might have fallen or been overtaken with sudden infirmity. After expressing her concern to neighbor Harry Beasley, the two hurried to Potter's farm to inquire after Walton. Potter, who had hired Walton the previous May to complete various projects on his land, told the two visitors that he had seen Walton working on the hedges just after noon, hard at work. Although he admitted to having passed within 600 feet of Walton, Potter said he did not hail his employee because he was hurrying to help a cow stuck in a ditch. Edith's growing apprehension contagious, the three rushed together to the spot Potter said he had last seen Walton at the top of a rise by the hedges, only to be met by a scene beyond horror.

Charles Walton crime scene

Edith began to scream hysterically, and Beasley took her back down the hill, worried not only about her emotional state but also that she might disturb the crime scene. Potter called out to a passerby, Harry Peachey, and Potter beseeched him to run for the police.

THE SCENE

Walton lay on the ground covered in blood. Someone had seemingly beaten him with his own walking stick, slit his throat with the slash hook and used the pitchfork to pin him to the ground by the neck. Both the pitchfork and the slash hook still lay in Walton's body, the hook buried in his throat along with the tines from the pitchfork. The pitchfork was embedded with such vehemence that it eventually required two officers to pry it from the ground. The handle of the pitchfork was jammed into the hedge to hold it in place. His walking stick lay just a few yards away, covered with blood and hair.

Potter said that Walton needed to finish only between six and ten yards of work when their paths crossed at approximately 12:10 that day. Walton had cut through about an additional four yards, which would have taken him about a half hour to complete, so officials determined the attack ensued just after 12:30 based on Potter's account. The killer opened Watson's shirt and unbuttoned his fly but did not further disrobe the man. Watson's pocket watch, valued at perhaps three months' wages for a typical working man at the time, was missing. Although officers later combed the area with metal detectors, the watch could not be located.

The autopsy disclosed that although the murderer struck Watson in the head, likely in an attempt to incapacitate him, the victim fought for his life. The back of his right hand and arm bore bruises, and his left hand was cut.

Police hoped the implements would yield fingerprints but were unable to recover any. The local superintendent of police, Alec Spooner, ran the initial investigation but soon felt the need for support from Scotland Yard. Detective Superintendent Robert Fabian, an officer renowned for his prowess, and an assistant, Sergeant Albert Webb, received the call and hurried to Warwickshire to help with the inquiry, arriving on February 16.

Modern slash hook

THE SUSPECTS

The Village

Amazingly, Fabian and Webb interviewed the entire village of Lower Quinton, asking all the inhabitants to explain their movements during the day in question. Although the population added up to fewer than 500 people, the undertaking must have been rather daunting, underlying the concern with which the police were eyeing the crime. Fabian placed an oversized map on the wall of the police station and used pushpins to indicate where the inhabitants supposedly were during the time of the murder. Unfortunately, this method apparently garnered no real suspects.

The Italian

Just a few days after Walton's death, police arrested an Italian prisoner of war from the nearby holding camp. A tipster told police a bloody man was hiding in the area, so they swooped in, sure they had their man. Although the Italian's hands clearly had blood on them, the interrogation revealed that he often found his way out of the camp to kill rabbits to supplement his meager diet.

Although technically a prison camp, the inmates there could come and go rather easily, and the camp administrators kept no records of which prisoners were there on which days and at which times. Although the local police did arrest this one prisoner, apparently no officials considered him a serious suspect even though the reasons for this attitude are no longer clear. It seems that perhaps officials checked the prisoners perhaps only to placate the locals. Potter might have echoed the feeling of many village residents by claiming the murderer must be one of the "fascists" from there, as no wholesome denizen would commit such an act.

Alfred Potter

Being the last person to admit seeing Walton alive, Potter himself quickly became a person of interest in the case. Potter said he had known Walton for about five years and found his employee to be an "inoffensive type of man," so he could not imagine who might want to murder him. After supposedly seeing Walton at work shortly after noon, Potter claimed to stopped at his home at 12:40 and then gone on to attend to the heifer.

Potter's alibi supported his claim of innocence. His wife assured police that he arrived home shortly after 12:30, read the newspaper for a few minutes and then gone off to assist a friend for less than half an hour while waiting for lunch. The friend confirmed Potter's presence with him from about 12:45 to shortly after 1 o'clock.

He also appeared to have no motive to kill Walton. Although some employees said Potter sometimes had difficulty coming up with their pay and Potter insinuated that Walton might have cheated him by exaggerating the number of hours he worked, the police did not consider a wage dispute an appropriate causative factor in the crime.

Some of Potter's story led police to question him more closely, however. For one thing, he and his wife both became overly excited when they heard police had arrested one of the Italians, making Fabian wonder at his exuberance. The most compelling concern was instead the fingerprint evidence. Nearly a week after the murder, an officer mentioned to Potter that they were still hoping to retrieve fingerprints from the murder weapons. Upon hearing this, Potter admitted he had handled at least one and perhaps both of the items when first discovering Walton, fearing the killer still lurked in the area. It turned out that no usable prints were recovered, but Potter's actions seemed bizarre to the Fabian.

In the long run, insufficient evidence to pursue Potter as the killer emerged, and he was never detained in the case.

Witchcraft

Webb believed only a "maniac" would attack an old man from behind with such vehemence, but Spooner conveyed his own theory, a suggestion that led the case into the annals of occultism. Fabian writes that Spooner pulled out a book for Fabian, showing the famed detective that another murder had taken place in exactly the same way 70 years earlier. A local man had allegedly attacked a woman, Ann Tennant, out of the blue, stabbing her repeatedly, eventually leaving her with a slashed throat and impaled by a pitchfork. The killer, John Hayward, told the court he killed the woman because she was a witch. Although he was supposedly found guilty of murder and eventually hanged, the legend of the murder lived on, with some residents believing Hayward might have been right. The author of the book Spooner referenced, a local named Clive Holland, asserted that the manner of the woman's death was consistent with the only effective way to kill a witch and keep her from returning from the beyond.

A vicar from the township had written a book, published in 1929, that related a story that caught Spooner's interest, as well. The story goes that just 10 years after the woman's gruesome pitchfork death, a young boy found himself confronted by a huge black dog – known locally as a Black Shuck, an ill omen – on his way home from work. He encountered the dog nine days in a row, and on the ninth day, a headless woman appeared with the creature. The connection to the 1945 case lay in the youth's name: Charles Walton.

Fabian initially discounted the theory but revisited it as the case grew cold. Investigating the history of death associated with witchcraft, he discovered that February 14 aligned with the Julian calendar date of February 2, considered the best day to commit a blood sacrifice to support the next year's harvest. Upon asking the local populace about the theory, he found few willing to discuss the issue, seemingly content to leave Walton's murder unsolved. Some hinted that Walton might have dabbled in witchcraft, but Fabian did not obtain detail to support such allegations. These attitudes gave Fabian pause, making him consider the blood sacrifice possibility seriously. With no real evidence for it, however, he was eventually forced to return to London without solving the killing.

FINAL THOUGHTS

Without full access to the records from the time, modern researchers may find it difficult to understand why police so readily abandoned the Italian prisoners as suspects in Walton's murder. Potter's behavior in touching the murder weapons might have been a bit strange in retrospect, but the shock upon finding a body in such condition and the fear that the perpetrator might still be in the area give reasonability to his attempt to grab the slash hook, at least. Since Beasley's motive in moving Edith away was in part to keep the scene intact, touching the slash hook seems particularly odd, but Potter had no clear motive and little or no opportunity to make such a vicious attack and then return to his normal routine without arousing suspicion.

A search of internet message boards indicates that most people familiar with the case today, including those living in Lower Quinton, believe Potter likely killed Walton in a dispute over money. Speculation exists that Walton lent Potter some cash, which accounts for both Walton's dwindling bank account and Potter's willingness to hire the older man who admittedly refused to work in the rain. Perhaps Walton began to pressure Potter for repayment since his account was running dangerously low, and Potter, who clearly had no extra money lying around, felt killing him his only option. Since no single withdrawal from Walton's account was larger than about a month's wages, however, the debtor theory, regardless of who might have received the money, fails to hold up strongly. In its defense, the police files finger Potter as the only true suspect.

The witchcraft theory is less credible. Although Ann Tennant was indeed killed, Hayward's crime bore little resemblance to Walton's murder except for the fact that the killers used a pitchfork. Hayward apparently possessed a low IQ and perhaps mental illness, which could account for his actions. Rather than being hanged, the court found him not guilty by reason of insanity, and he lived out the final years of his life in an asylum.

Additionally, the Charles Walton from the vicar's story may likely be a different boy. The details about the boy's family don't match up with this Walton's life, making it difficult to determine the boy's true identity. Even if the story were true and about the same person, the connection between this hellish experience as a youth and the violent murder 70 years later seems weak at best.

Fabian's writings later in his life emphasize the cold attitude of the townspeople and their reluctance to share information for the investigation, leading him to conclude that people were hiding what really happened that Valentine's Day. However, published nearly a decade after Walton's death, who can say why people did not speak up more readily. Is it truly more likely that they were hiding a secret about blood rituals and witchcraft or that they had no information to add?

Fabian also recounts his own spooky encounter just before leaving the village. As he walked the hills, a black dog ran by him. A young boy shortly appeared, and Fabian asked if the boy was looking for the dog. Upon hearing that the creature was black, Fabian claims the boy turned pale and tore down the hill in the opposite direction. The inspector says he later found a black dog hanging from a tree. Whether true or not, this tale emphasizes the superstitious air of the townsfolk at the time and Fabian's later mindset about Walton's death.

With modern techniques such as profiling, readers may also wonder why the police did not consider Edith a suspect. Walton's savings dwindled at a pace faster than it reasonably should have given his supplemental income from labor and his frugal living conditions. Edith's beau at the time, Edgar Goode, provided a satisfying account of himself during the period in question, but police records do not indicate how well they checked out that alibi. Although he and Edith had apparently been dating for several years and she was of marriageable age – her early thirties – why had they not taken the next step? Had she perhaps been culling money from her adopted father's/uncle's accounts and she found someone to kill him when the money was nearly gone in order to keep him from finding out? No evidence exists now to point the finger at Edith, but neither does any evidence illustrate that police pursued and eliminated the possibility.

Edith stands out as a possibility because of a discovery in the 1960s. Some twenty years after the murder, the outhouses behind what had been Walton's home were being torn down when a worker discovered an old tin watch, later determined to be the very one Walton supposedly took with him that fateful day. If correctly identified, how did the timepiece make its way back to Walton's property? Supposedly, police scoured that area after the killing, so the killer must have returned the watch to the building afterward. Who would do so, and why? Some may speculate that Edith placed it there while others might believe the murderer risked the return to avoid some sort of bad luck or curse following him because of it. Easily identifiable and not particularly valuable, the watch was not an easy item to profit from.

In the end, it does seem robbery to be at least the secondary motive. It is easy to picture the killer tearing open Walton's shirt and checking down his pants for a hidden pocket, ending up taking the only object on his person: his watch. An elderly man standing alone by the hedge would seem an easy target if only his tools could be wrested from him. The attack from behind and the fact that Walton was killed with only the objects upon his person seem to indicate an impulse attack rather than a planned murder, consistent with a young, inexperienced attacker who did not expect his victim to put up such a struggle. Unfortunately, blood sacrifices for favorable crops and witchcraft rituals are not necessary motives for murder.

Chapter 3: Julia Wallace, Anfield, Liverpool

January, 1931

THE DISCOVERY

William Wallace left his wife of 18 years, Julia, at about 6:30 pm on Tuesday, January 20 to meet with a potential client. A salesman for Prudential Insurance, Wallace seldom held evening meetings. However, he hated to turn down the possible commission from a sale and so planned to meet the Mr. Qualtrough who had left a message at Wallace's club the previous night. Wallace embarked on a series of trains looking for the address in question – 25 Melove Gardens East – but encountered difficulty finding it. After inquiring at numerous stops and of several people along the way, including a policeman, Wallace finally gave up his search about an hour and a half later and hurried home.

A local milk-boy and a newspaper girl both verified that Julia appeared alive and well at approximately the time her husband left on his adventure, having answered the door to speak to the milk-boy. Although the young man placed the time of his encounter at 6:30, the girl who noticed the conversation estimated the time about 15 minutes later. Either way, it remains unclear if William had already departed.

Upon arrival at home after his snipe hunt, Wallace used his key at the front door as usual but found the bolt pulled, making entry impossible. Confused and growing increasingly anxious at receiving no reply from the darkened house, he moved to the back door but found it locked tight, as well. Thinking perhaps that the front lock had been sticking, as it often did, he tried there again with no luck. As he trekked to the back door yet again, he ran into his neighbors, the Johnstons, to whom he explained his concerns. In answer to his query, they claimed to have not heard or seen anything suspicious during the previous few hours, but Wallace bemoaned his inability to get into the house. Some nearby houses had been burglarized in the recent weeks, so the party grew concerned about the possibility of a break-in.

The Johnstons suggested Wallace try the back again, and this time the door opened as they watched from just outside the yard. The couple waited there as Wallace went through the house to look for his wife, lighting the gas bulbs as he went through the kitchen, up the stairs to the bedroom. Since Julia had been ill, he thought perhaps she had turned in early. Not finding her there, he hurried back down the stairs and to the front room where he at last found her, although not in the condition he expected. He called for the Johnstons, and Mr. Johnston hastened off to find an officer.

THE SCENE

Julia lay by the unlit gas fireplace in a pool of blood. Blood spattered the walls and furniture in the room. The force used had split open her skull and exposed the brain. The coroner later announced the assailant struck her head 11 times even though the first blow caused her to fall and would have been sufficient to kill her. He also determined she died at about 6 pm, an impossibility given the milk-boy and paper girl's testimony, but at least the timing indicates the murder took place early in the evening rather than after Wallace returned to the house.

Underneath her body lay her husband's raincoat, also covered with blood. Though the fire was out, her dress was scorched. Although accounts from the time fail to explain when he noticed it, Wallace showed the Johnstons that a cabinet in the kitchen had been wrenched open, within which typically lay the insurance payments Wallace had collected; it was empty.

No other signs of break-in appeared in the house. Wallace said he believed he had unbolted the front door to let the police in, which was contrary to the couple's normal routine. When Wallace left in the evenings, he would go out the back and Julia would pull the bolt behind him, leaving the front door unbolted so he could use his key to get in. Police also found no obvious weapon although the fireplace poker and the iron cleaning bar were missing.

Julia Wallace crime scene

THE SUSPECTS

Qualtrough

Wallace insisted he left the house that evening to meet with the unfamiliar Mr. Qualtrough who had asked for an appointment at 25 Menlove Gardens East. A worker at Wallace's club took the message the previous evening before Wallace showed up. The caller requested Wallace meet with him at 7:30 the next night.

Since no such address existed, police had no way of finding the caller. The worker, who knew Wallace well from the club, insisted the caller was not a familiar voice and could not have been confused with Wallace, and nobody recognized the name. It did not take long before police decided Qualtrough did not exist and was instead a ruse cooked up by the murderer to get Wallace out of the house or by Wallace himself to create an alibi.

Random Robber

Since the killer apparently took money from the hideaway cupboard, officials explored the possibility of robbery as a motive. The total stolen amounted to relatively little (about $1,000 in today's terms). Wallace admitted to regular habits regarding deposits: he usually banked funds on Wednesdays, making him a target for a Tuesday evening robbery. This particular week's funds were more meager than many others, but people certainly do rob others for less, and the killer had no way of knowing exactly how much was in the house.

The absence of forced entry caused some to discount this theory, although the killer could have feigned an appointment with Wallace and gained access; Julia might have allowed a stranger to wait in the parlor for her husband's return. The murderer simply would wait until her back was turned and then pounce, take the money and leave.

The problem with this possibility lies in the logistics. Times were different then, and Julia certainly might have opened her home to a potential client. However, a robber (or murderer) seemingly would take a weapon with him rather than use the fireplace tools. If those items were not used to batter Julia, why did they disappear? Why risk removing the items from the house? If this unknown killer sent Wallace on the wild Qualtrough chase, he would know Julia would stay home. What did he expect to do with her? If he expected to murder her, why the ploy to get her husband out of the house?

The house appeared orderly except for the one kitchen cupboard and the bloody scene in the front room, indicating the thief knew where to find the cash. A random robber could not be privy to such information.

William Wallace

Police settled on Wallace as the clearest suspect, and seemingly rightly so. His convenient absence from the club when Qualtrough called, queries regarding the address in the club upon receiving the message, constant questioning of people along his route and noting of the time and inability to enter the house at first all seem dubious.

The coroner's estimated time of Julia's death means Wallace could have killed her just before leaving. Although tight, the timing makes him a viable possibility since the neither the milk-boy nor Wallace could attest to his presence in the home at that time, and no witnesses came forward to say they saw when Wallace actually departed.

The couple carried little life insurance on Julia, making the policy a weak motive for her husband to have killed her, and the couple seemed reserved yet devoted to each other, electing to spend time alone rather than in many social circles. William had his chess club but no intrigue there or elsewhere surfaced during the investigation.

Officials arrested Wallace for the murder February 2, perhaps largely because they found no other suspect. The defense presented the witnesses along Wallace's route as evidence of innocence while prosecutors used the same witnesses and testimony as evidence of a guilty man establishing an alibi. The defense insisted the perpetrator would be drenched in blood, but the prosecution countered that the killer clearly wore the raincoat during the attack (though they failed to explain how the killer placed the coat beneath the body without getting further covered in blood).

The lack of motive bothered many associated with the case, and in the end, the judge summed up by emphasizing that lack along with the contradictory evidence meant the jury should acquit. However, they convicted Wallace in short order. Wallace's attorney won an appeal, saying the conviction ran contrary to the evidence, and Wallace went free. He died just a couple years later, proclaiming his innocence to the end.

Richard Gordon Parry

But the case did not die with William Wallace. Nearly 40 years later, writer Jonathan Goodman suggested another prospect, a former coworker of Wallace's who might have held a grudge.

Richard Gordon Parry worked with Wallace at Prudential for a time prior to the murder. Apparently, Wallace reported Parry's alleged misappropriation of funds to the company, and Parry got fired. Rumors abounded at the time that Parry and Julia Wallace became romantically involved despite the 30-odd-year age difference. Even if no such trysting occurred, Parry clearly possessed motive to hurt Wallace.

Although Wallace at first claimed to be stymied regarding any possible suspects, he presented the police with a list of prospective killers the day after Julia's death. Among the names was Richard Gordon Parry. However, police cleared Parry due to an alibi provided by his girlfriend, and police returned to Wallace as the best suspect.

FINAL THOUGHTS

Preparing for a radio program in the early 1980s, researcher Roger Wilkes rediscovered Parry's girlfriend. Fifty years after first giving Parry an alibi, she at that point denied that Parry stayed with her the entire evening. The theory of Parry as the killer also gets support from a statement from one of Parry's acquaintances, John Parkes, who worked cleaning cars at the time of the murder. Parkes says Parry insisted his car get washed both inside and out, and Parkes found a bloody glove. He claims Parry snatched the article away and exclaimed, "If the police found that, it would hang me!"

This possibility remains the most intriguing, even without the late support from Parry's girlfriend and Parkes. The Qualtrough story creates a somewhat bumbling alibi for Wallace; one might expect such a master criminal to come up with a clearer window for himself if possible along with a more common name to make the story more believable. Julia would likely allow Parry in the house, and the bludgeoning of the face and head points to a personal cause for the killing. Parry might also have known about the money's hiding place in the house, particularly if he and Julia truly had a relationship.

The story makes more sense if someone – either Parry or someone with a similar need to get back at Wallace – wanted to frame Wallace for the murder.

The situation of the doors remains a conundrum, however. Why did the back door suddenly open for Wallace after he had already tried it? Could the killer have been waiting inside for a chance to escape, running out after Wallace tried the back and returned to the front of the house? If so, why wouldn't the Johnstons have spied the person leaving?

At any rate, famed detective novelist and screenwriter Raymond Chandler summed up the case well by saying, "I call it the impossible murder because Wallace couldn't have done it, and neither could anyone else."

Chapter 4: Jane Stanford, Oahu, Hawaii

February, 1905

THE DISCOVERY

Jane Lathrop Stanford, widow of Leland Stanford and co-founder of the university bearing their name, had reached the age of 76 in January of 1905 when someone attempted to poison her.

While at home, she took a drink of mineral water that did not agree with her. The bitter taste so worried her that she forced herself to vomit. She asked both her maid Elizabeth Richmond and her private secretary Bertha Berner to taste the drink. Since all women agreed the water tasted exceedingly ascerbic, Stanford sent the bottle to the Harry Morse Detective Agency to have it tested for poison, which came back positive.

Understandably upset at the idea that someone in her home tried to kill her, Stanford abandoned the mansion. Apparently at Morse's suggestion, Stanford dismissed Richmond since she seemed the prime suspect. The maid had entered Stanford's employ only recently while Bertha Berner had been with the Stanfords for at least two decades, making Richmond the more plausible suspect of the two. Morse seemingly felt one of the two women most likely responsible since they had easy access to Stanford.

Late the next month, nursing a nasty cold, Stanford decided to trek to Hawaii and stay at the Moana Hotel. Feeling the effects of the illness in her stomach, she asked Berner to prepare a sodium bicarbonate. After consuming the drink, instead of soothing her stomach, Stanford found that she could not control her body and called out for assistance, insisting she had again been poisoned.

The summoned physician, Dr. Francis Humphris, found himself thwarted in his attempts to help Stanford since the elderly woman complained of pain and stiffness in her jaw, making swallowing the concoction he fixed for her difficult. She then began to spasm until her body became completely rigid, at which point she stopped breathing, dying that Friday night, February 28.

THE SCENE

The medication Stanford had ingested was tested and found to contain strychnine, the same fatal poison previously discovered in the mineral water at her home. The sodium bicarbonate administered by the secretary had apparently travelled with them from California, meaning anyone with access to the house could have tampered with it. This night in February marked the first time anyone used the package since the move out of the mansion.

Upon Stanford's death, the doctors collected all the material in her room for analysis, including the glass with the sodium bicarb, the package it came from, the spoon used to stir it, the waste she had expelled and a few cascara capsules (made from bark of a tree used as a natural laxative) on her bedtable. No other items contained strychnine or any other substance that might account for Stanford's symptoms and ultimate death.

Strychnine poisoning results in an agonizing demise. Absorbing quickly into the bloodstream and organs, ingesting raises blood pressure and may lead to cardiac arrest. Intense convulsions typically occur along with respiratory difficulties. Although colorless, the powder has a bitter taste. These symptoms certainly go hand-in-hand with Stanford's symptoms and Dr. Humphris's observation.

A jury swiftly returned the unsurprising verdict just days later verifying that Mrs. Stanford had died of poison. Newspapers throughout the country had already announced to all and sundry that she had been murdered.

Leland Stanford Jr. Museum, ~1900

THE SUSPECTS

David Starr Jordan

David Jordan, President of Stanford University at the time, immediately went into damage control mode upon Mrs. Stanford's death. Apparently fearing that murder would hurt the school's reputation, he flew to Hawaii, hired his own doctor to investigate the cause of death and began hinting that a conspiracy was taking place.

Jordan's hired physician, Dr. Timothy Hopkins, proclaimed the woman actually succumbed to heart failure. Prompted by Jordan's statements, even powerful newspapers like the *New York Times* ran stories suggesting that the jury's verdict came without proper support and therefore hastily – and incorrectly – reached. He wrote to the Stanford Board of Trustees, listing a number of possible causes of natural death including heart failure.

However, just a few weeks later, several doctors (Dr. Wood, Dr. Humphris and Dr. Murray) announced again their firm belief that Stanford died from strychnine poisoning. In support of their contention came a statement from a "chemist" (roughly equivalent to a modern pharmacist), Edmund Shorey. As an educational leader, Jordan's words received more credence than those of Hawaii's doctors in the eyes of the university administration and much of the public. Jordan also literally accused Humphris of putting the strychnine into the medication after Stanford died, accounting for the findings by the other physicians but still allowing the possibility of a heart attack as the cause of death.

Interestingly, after Hopkins filed his report and Humphris called him on the carpet for his unprofessionalism on the case, Hopkins met with a lawyer, took payment for his work from Jordan and left the country.

Jordan's potential motive came out upon examination of the relationship between himself and Stanford long after the public accepted the story of Stanford's death by heart attack. At the time of her death, she served as the head of the board of trustees, the group responsible for selecting the school's president, and the rumor was that Jordan was on his way out because of Stanford. Modern researcher Dr. Robert Cutler writes that evidence shows Stanford trying to gather support to fire the President. Apparently Stanford managed to get a faculty member to collect information about Jordan in his daily work, a man who was immediately fired when Stanford died. That instructor, Professor Goebel, wrote shortly before Stanford's death that the founder had decided Jordan had to go for the good of the institution. Holding on to such a prestigious and well-paying position certainly sounds like motive, but investigators seemingly accepted Jordan's assertion of Stanford's natural death, eliminating him as a potential person of interest in a murder.

Bertha Berner

Berner seems a plausible suspect primarily due to proximity: she was the only person with Stanford in both California and Hawaii; she clearly had close, personal access to her employer; and she mixed the fatal sodium bicarbonate dose.

Many modern sleuths point out Berner's long relationship with Stanford, given alternatively at 20 or 30 years, as evidence for her exoneration. A long-time relationship fails to stand up on its own as very powerful support, however.

Other staff members told officials that Berner seemed to genuinely care for her employer. Stanford left Berner well cared-for in her will, giving her 15 times what the other household members received, amounting to about $100,000 in today's terms, along with a home. Inheritance has historically created powerful motive for murder, enough that police considered Berner a potential suspect for a short time but quickly dismissed due to her close relationship with Stanford.

FINAL THOUGHTS

The first issue to put to bed lies in the question of murder. Regardless of the later commentary based on Jordan's spin, even a cursory look at Humphris's account of the symptoms that evening point toward an unnatural death, and the previous undisputed attempt of strychnine poisoning makes Stanford's eventual death through the same means more plausible. Her symptoms, particularly the spasms, simply do not match that of a heart attack brought on by age.

Although Berner seems the obvious suspect to murder Stanford, she actually seems a bit too obvious. Only a very obtuse killer would put herself in the position of having administered the fatal dose rather than providing herself an alibi or even allowing for another likely suspect. Stanford herself clearly felt Berner incapable of being the culprit in the first attempted poisoning, a telling point about the relationship between the women.

The fact that Stanford died in Hawaii six weeks after the California poisoning lends little support to the Berner theory since the sodium bicarbonate packet came from the house. Any person with access to the mansion could have tampered with the medication, knowing Stanford would eventually ingest it.

Potentially, the maid Elizabeth Richmond could therefore have actually put the strychnine in the medication at the same time as the mineral water. The reason for Richmond to kill Stanford remains vague, however. Since she stood to inherit some money upon Stanford's death, she could possibly be the culprit, but this motive appears rather anemic since the amount would not have been huge, and she could not have felt guaranteed to receive anything since she was new to the employ.

Jordan's quick (and successful) attempts to cover up the murder arouse suspicion. Given the strained relationship between the two, the scenario of Jordan being invited to Stanford's home and finding the opportunity to slip strychnine into two different substances rings rather incredible. Using a servant in the mansion, such as the relatively new maid, raises tantalizing possibilities. The timing of Stanford's death as it relates to Jordan's potential dismissal enhances his position as a suspect. But what if she had waited longer than six weeks to need the sodium bicarbonate? Perhaps the timing comes from coincidence, after all.

A random poisoner can be ruled out since the two very different items contained strychnine: both the mineral water and the sodium bicarbonate. Clearly, Stanford became a target. The question remains who had both motive and opportunity.

Chapter 5: Gruber/Baumgartner, Hinterkaifeck, Bavaria

March, 1922

THE DISCOVERY

On Thursday, March 30, 1922, farmer Andreas Gruber reported a break-in on his isolated property near the Bavarian town of Kaifeck to his neighbor Lorenz Schlittenbauer and a friend named Kaspar Stegmair. Gruber, aged 63, lived in the house cradled by the woods with his wife Cazilia, nearly a decade older than her husband; their widowed daughter Victoria Gabriel, aged 35; and Victoria's children Cazilia (called Cilli), 7; and Josef, 2. (Although reports variously present Cilli's age as 7, 9 and 11, given the date her parents wed, 7 seems the most likely.) Gruber supposedly said footprints of two men clearly led through the blanket of newly-fallen snow up to the engine house, but none appeared to show the perpetrators leaving the area. Since the trespassers took nothing and apparently simply broke the lock on the building housing the family vehicles, Gruber failed to make an official report to police. Stegmair's son later recounted his father's tale to the officials, wherein Gruber allegedly told Stegmair he knew the intruders must have broken in and stayed somewhere on the property since he found no prints leaving the farm. When Stegmair implored the elderly man to leave the area so the invaders could be searched for, Gruber tossed his head, insisting he felt no fear about the situation.

Late afternoon the next day, Friday, the Grubers' new maid, Maria Baumgartner, arrived at the house along with her sister. The previous maid had left the Grubers' employ the previous September, allegedly claiming the house contained ghosts. Maria sent her sister off an hour later and settled in for her new duties.

Saturday dawned silently over the farm. At that time in the area, children attended school on Saturdays, but little Cilli did not appear that day. Although nobody apparently checked on the household from the school, two men did knock on the Grubers' door between noon and 2 pm but received no answer. A local man noted lights on and smoke from the chimney at the house when he passed it that evening but said in his initial statement that he saw no one in particular.

Sunday worshippers missed the Grubers at church, but no visitors from the neighboring area were able to rouse a response at the farm. Still not thinking anything terribly amiss, nobody reported the family's absence to authorities or searched the property.

On Monday, the postman left the paper on the kitchen window as usual but noted the baby's absence. He said he nearly always spied the boy lying in his carriage in the kitchen when he delivered to the house. However, nothing otherwise seemed out of place. Cilli again failed to show up at school. Her absence noted, no one raised an alarm.

Workman Albert Hoffner arrived at the homestead promptly at 9 am on Tuesday, April 4, to work on an engine. Finding no one at home and the back door closed and locked, he waited in the garden area for about an hour, thinking Gruber had stepped out. He could hear the family dog barking from inside the house when he first arrived. Lounging in the shade of the apple tree, he occasionally whistled during his wait to alert the residents of his presence but hailed nobody.

Feeling pressed for time, Hoffner eventually pushed open the garage and began repairing the engine, whistling and singing as he worked, thinking to alert the family that he was there when they returned home. Finishing up about 2:30 pm, he walked back through the garden area and noted the dog now tied up outside the house. Surprised the Grubers had failed to hear the racket he was making during his work, Hoffner tried the front door but found it locked, as well. Leaving the property, he hailed Schlittenbauer, who lived only about 1/4 of a mile away from the Grubers, and told the neighbor of the eerie silence about the place.

Schlittenbauer sent his two sons to see whom they could find at the Gruber farm. They soon returned, reporting the same condition Hoffner had noted: the dog tied just outside the house but no other signs of life and no obvious portents of danger.

Growing more concerned, perhaps remembering Gruber's comment about the footprints in the snow, Schlittenbauer roused two other neighbors, Poll and Sigl, and returned to Gruber's farm along with his own sons. About 90 minutes passed between the time the boys checked on the family to when the group of men appeared. Upon reaching the farm, the boys pointed out that the dog had been moved yet again, but no people seemed to be in the area. Since the pet's barking at that point came from the barn, the three older men entered the building, leaving the boys to watch the yard. The door to the barn was closed but clearly broken, allowing the men entry to the scene out of a modern horror film.

THE SCENE

The bodies of Andreas, his wife Cazilia, Victoria and the child Cilli lay sprawled among the hay in the barn. Blood pooled along the floor and soaked into the hay. Schlittenbauer noted Gruber's head pushed up against the brick side of the building had clearly been bludgeoned, even in the gloom of the unlit barn. As his eyes adjusted, he could see more bodies in the hay and pulled them out from the material to more easily see who they were, moving the women in the process. It is unclear from statements where exactly the dog was tethered in the building.

The coroner later determined that the murderer had struck Cilli several times in the face, and she suffered a serious neck wound. Her clenched fists held clumps of her own hair, which she had yanked out in her death throes. Horrifyingly, the coroner believed she might have lived for as long as three hours after the attack.

Cazilia endured a skull fracture as a result of seven strikes to the head with a heavy object. Both her and Cilli's skulls showed circular wounds, resembling the damage a hammer might cause, but the coroner later determined the other injuries likely caused by something like a pickaxe. The right side of Andreas's face had been obliterated during the onslaught.

Victoria, however, sustained the brunt of the attack. The killer hit her on the head no fewer than nine times; she bore that number of star-shaped holes in her skull. The coroner uses the term "smashed" when describing her skull. In addition to this trauma, she had been strangled.

Victoria had named Schlittenbauer as father to her baby, so he became particularly anxious to find the child and see if he was still alive. Poll and Sigl remained just outside the doorway but followed Schlittenbauer to the house. Schlittenbauer apparently used a key, although accounts do not explain if he already had it or if he took it from the barn or another hiding place, and entered the home.

In Victoria's bedroom, they encountered the baby carriage. The shuttered windows mercifully shadowed the horrific scene. The killer had swung a heavy implement through the canopy and into the baby's head, destroying both the cover and the young life in one blow, striking the infant in the head. The room otherwise was neatly made up – the bed made and no signs of ransacking. Josef's unused crib sat in a lonely corner behind the door.

Maria slumped on the floor of the crowded servant's room, her still-full backpack on a bench under one of the small windows. Her shoes peeked out from a heavy quilt, which the men lifted. Her head had also been bashed in.

Poll and Sigl left to get the police while Schlittenbauer stayed at the scene. His presence might have preserved evidence since people from the area began to appear and poke through the farm, ogling the carnage. Only when officials arrived at about 6:15 were looky-loos kept off the property. The investigation into the murders had to wait for detectives from Munich, who got to the mayor's house that Tuesday at about midnight but waited until the next morning to visit the scene.

The officials took photos of the house and surrounding area Wednesday morning, after which the coroner, Dr. Johann Aumuller, performed the autopsies in the barn.

THE SUSPECTS

Random Robbery

Many speculated that the household fell victim to thieves who had secreted themselves on the property for the several days before and after the killings. Several clues support this contention, such as the footprints Gruber allegedly mentioned the day prior to the murders, the apparent lack of motive for the slaughter and the rumors regarding the condition of the attic after the deaths.

Stories circulated that the floor of the attic was covered with a layer of straw, seemingly to muffle the footsteps of the perpetrator(s) hiding there. Supposedly, two piles of straw looked suspiciously like beds, bacon rinds were found, and some even espoused the understanding that piles of human feces were found. Such evidence certainly makes it seem that someone lived in the attic, and one would have no reason to muffle footsteps after the family was already dead. An acquaintance of Gruber's named Bley later told investigators that Andreas confided to him that he heard odd noises coming from the attic during the night of Thursday, March 30 but could not find the source.

Even without taking the stories regarding the condition of the attic into consideration, the evidence clearly demonstrates at least one person was alive on the property after the murders. The smoke and lights seen on Saturday, the movements of the dog on Tuesday and the fact that someone tended the livestock between Saturday and Tuesday lead to this conclusion.

But what kind of thief worries about taking care of the animals after killing the inhabitants of the farm? The biggest counter to the robbery motive comes from the fact that investigators found money – the equivalent of about $2000 today – around the house in addition to jewelry, bonds, animals, equipment and ammunition, as well, none so cleverly concealed that anyone looking even in a cursory manner should have found it.

In addition, the descriptions of the attic with its bedding and footstep-muffling floor do not come until 1952, 30 years after the murders. They cannot represent newly-discovered information at that point since relatives tore down the property in the 1920s. Bley did not tell his story of Andreas's "odd noises" tale until 1930, reducing the credibility.

Police abandoned the robbery theory early in the investigation because of the amount of money found in the house.

Karl Gabriel

Although she had been a widow for over seven years, Victoria's husband Karl Gabriel became a suspect for a time. Supposedly killed in action during World War I, he nonetheless aroused suspicion since his body was not returned to his family for burial. However, several soldiers serving with Karl who knew him well saw him fall in battle and verified that he could not have killed the people at Hinterkaifeck.

Lorenz Schlittenbauer

Police looked at Schlittenbauer, as well, presumably because of his relationship with Victoria. He said Victoria first propositioned him shortly after hearing of her husband's death in 1914 but that he turned her down because he was married at the time. His wife later passed away in the middle of 1918, after which he took Victoria up on her offer, he said, having sex no more than half a dozen times over the subsequent two and a half years. He told interrogators that he and Victoria both wanted to marry but that her father forbade it.

When she had baby Josef in 1919, Victoria listed Schlittenbauer as the father, a charge he at first denied. Just a couple weeks later, however, he acknowledged paternity and agreed in court to pay child support. He claimed he again broached the subject of marriage but was rebuffed by Gruber. (Schlittenbauer remarried in July of 1921 to a woman he had known only three weeks, apparently giving up on the idea of wedding Victoria.)

Schlittenbauer's actions upon finding the bodies aroused suspicion in some of the locals. The men who discovered the bloody scene with him puzzled over Schlittenbauer's movements. Sigl told police in his initial statement that Schlittenbauer suggested they feed the cattle, at which Sigl logically stated he thought it more important to leave the scene unchanged and contact police. Schlittenbauer agreed but then moved immediately to the basement to get milk for the pigs. Sigl expressed his surprise that Schlittenbauer found the tools and feed unhesitatingly, a shock since everyone knew the two men did not get along well.

Others felt Schlittenbauer a suspect, as well. Poll agreed with Sigl's account, adding to the concern by discussing the family dog's personality in more detail. Poll stated that the dog performed well as a watchdog, speculating about who would have been able to kill the family and move the dog with such ease. Nearly a decade after the murders, a man by the name of Plockl claimed he saw Schlittenbauer manning a large fire and said he was sure the man burned bloodstained clothes that night. In addition, just after his son's bloody death, Schlittenbauer petitioned the court to see if he could obtain a refund for his final support payment, a request the court denied.

Although police interrogated Schlittenbauer again in 1931 and found his story somewhat contradictory to his initial statement and the facts of the case, they did not arrest him and dropped their investigation into him.

Adolf and Anton Gump

The Gump brothers entered the investigation in 1952 when their dying sister told her priest she believed them guilty of the killings. The local prosecutor at the time, a man named Popp, suggested Adolf had been intimately involved with Victoria and, enraged with jealousy after the birth of little Josef by another man, murdered the family.

Officials began searching in earnest for Adolf after suspecting him in a spate of robbery-murders in late 1921. They arrested Anton Gump in 1926, and he stood trial for fraud. At the time, police questioned him about the Hinterkaifeck killings but apparently gleaned no helpful information. However, his responses failed to exonerate him or his brother in Propp's eyes, and, three decades after the deaths on the farm, the prosecutor pursued the line of inquiry even though Adolf had died in 1944. Propp felt his evidence strong enough to take the surviving brother into custody.

The arrest of Anton Gump in 1952 might have closed the books on the Hinterkaifeck killings, but the prisoner gained release just over three weeks later since Germany had a 20-year statute of limitations on murder. The case against the Gumps seems to have been made up entirely of the deathbed statement of their sister, the suspicion they had killed others and the memory of a supposed statement from Sigl suggesting the brothers' complicity. The records including such accusations had long been destroyed, so prosecutors possessed no support for the charges.

The memorial to the victims at the site of the house.

FINAL THOUGHTS

Much of the speculation and confusion regarding this case stems from misinformation and accounts from years and, in some cases, decades, after the fact, confusing the facts. The police records make no mention of a mysterious newspaper belonging to nobody in the house, Victoria withdrawing her entire savings or distinct signs of human habitation in the attic. A close look at the initial firsthand accounts provides a clearer focus on what actually happened and what the most likely motive was for the murders.

The stories of intruders seem farfetched. In the tough economic climate of Germany in the early 1920s, the Grubers had a reputation as a family with money, making them seem a logical target. But what person would think trespassers had squatted on his property without taking action, particularly one with such property to protect, not to mention a family? Although Bley apparently possessed no reason to lie about the conversation with Gruber, his recollection was not recorded until 1930, plenty of time for confusion or confabulation. Besides Schlittenbauer, the only other corroboration for the intruders Gruber purportedly knew about comes secondhand, not from Stegmair but from his son who admittedly did not hear the conversation. And Schlittenbauer clearly does not make a reliable witness given his close association to the case.

Some consider the previous maid's contention that the house was haunted as evidence of intruders who had been living there for some time before killing the family. Since the woman quit in August of the previous year, that would require the murderer(s) to have hidden undetected for more than six months. The fact that she had a five-month-old child makes a more likely reason for the maid's departure. Even if she did tell Gruber ghosts chased her out, a story not corroborated by sources at the time, she might have lied to create a more plausible rationale.

The husband Karl Gabriel as the killer makes even less sense. What motive did he have? He abandoned his pregnant wife just four months after the wedding to join the army, but records fail to reveal if Gabriel volunteered or was conscripted. The only true evidence of an unhappy union comes from Jacob Sigl who admitted his impression was just that – an impression that did not stem from hard facts or firsthand accounts from either party in the marriage. Why then would Gabriel fake his death and wait over seven years to hack up not only his wife but her entire family and the new maid, including his own daughter? How would he manage to stay out of sight for so long both before and after the killings? Coupled with his comrades' assurances of his death in combat, Gabriel does not make a good suspect.

Not much information remains to explain the connection between the Gumps and Hinterkaifeck, creating a tantalizing mystery for the modern reader. But the autopsy reports indicate these men as not particularly credible suspects. The hacking of the family's faces, the single blow to the baby's head, the killing of the maid and the strangulation and overkill directed at Victoria point toward a personal cause killing focused on the young mother and perpetrated by someone who knew he had to kill everyone to avoid detection. Since no hard evidence regarding a liaison between Victoria and either Gump brother exists, it seems likely just a rumor. The most logical suspect is indeed Lorenz Schlittenbauer.

What motive did Schlittenbauer have? The paternity of young Josef. Killing the baby relieved him of that financial burden, even though he could afford the payments, and murdering both Victoria and Andreas would have been satisfying for a man livid over the situation of admitting he fathered the baby but not being allowed to marry the child's mother. Schlittenbauer gave evidence against Andreas and Victoria in an incest charge when the baby first arrived. Although he later withdrew his accusation, the charges stuck, and both Gruber and his daughter spent time in jail. It seems many local residents knew of the improper relationship between father and daughter, so it was no well-kept secret. Clearly, there was bad blood between the men.

If Schlittenbauer did kill Andreas and Victoria, he might have felt forced to murder the other adults and Cilla to avoid detection. Josef would have had to die to stop the paternity payments. Schlittenbauer's first thought, even before notifying the police about the bodies, was to feed the livestock. While such action could be construed as that of a compassionate, animal-loving individual, the killer(s) had obviously been caring for the stock over the weekend, creating a stronger connection to Schlittenbauer given his conduct. One might also expect a compassionate, caring person to be overcome with horror at the murders, especially that of the man's own young son.

One of the most compelling reasons to suspect Schlittenbauer besides his bizarre behavior upon finding the corpses is simple: the dog. Poll's testimony reveals that the dog would be unlikely to allow some random person to tie him in the various places witnesses saw him that Tuesday, but the hound clearly knew Schlittenbauer and so might have been more compliant.

Some may wonder what Schlittenbauer's wife had to say about his whereabouts in early April of 1922. No record indicates police interviewed her. But what might she have said? In what appears quite obviously an arranged marriage, it seems unlikely such a woman would have spoken out against her man. She could also have been completely unaware of his movements since her infant daughter, less than a month old, died of whooping cough on March 29 – an event a profiler might consider a trigger for a killer.

Chapter 6: Gareth Williams, London, England

August, 2010

THE DISCOVERY

Gareth Williams, aged 30, lived a James Bond life: he was, literally a spy. A gifted athlete and brilliant mathematician who graduated from Bangor University at the tender age of 17, MI6, the British spy service akin to the American CIA, eagerly sought out the young man who worked deciphering codes for the agency.

Although he kept largely to himself and did not have a large social circle, coworkers noted his absence from his job and asked authorities to perform a welfare check on August 23, 2010. The first hint at a cover-up comes upon the realization that the last affirmed sighting of Williams took place more than a week prior, on August 15.

A bizarre scene met police as they gained entry to the London apartment. Far from the splashes of blood and gore found at so many murder scenes, Williams' apartment appeared undisturbed according to first responders, his nude body folded neatly into a zippered and locked duffle bag in the bathroom.

THE SCENE

The large bag, padlocked from the outside, drew police attention. An autopsy gleaned no insight into Williams' death; his body contained no toxins, no alcohol or drugs, no signs of violence. It bore no marks showing he had been tied or forcefully gripped and thrust into the bag.

However, the inquiry experts determined he was most likely alive since putting a fresh kill into such a position would have been particularly difficult. The only marks borne on the body were small scratches on the elbows, inconsistent with someone forcing him into the position. The key to the padlock lay beneath the corpse inside the bag.

By the time Scotland Yard received the call and entered the residence, Williams' employers had been there and taken hold of property such as computer memory cards, fueling suggestions of a cover-up and perhaps compromising the investigation. At the very least, their presence certainly contaminated the scene.

Investigators found no outside fingerprints, footprints or other evidence of an intruder. In fact, they found no footprints anywhere in the bathroom nor any fingerprints on the bag or the padlock. This lack of physical evidence more than anything else prompted the coroner, Fiona Wilcox, to determine Williams the victim of murder.

THE SUSPECTS

MI6 or the CIA

Some, including many close to Williams, postulate that his own employer killed him, thinking him too much of a risk or for a breach in security. Five years after the death, an unnamed source from the security agency claimed Williams had pulled a guest list for a Bill Clinton event from the agency's computers for a friend, a serious violation of protocol.

This American connection is what makes some suspicious of the American spy agency. What else did he uncover during this computer hack? The thinking goes that even if he found no compromising information, his ability to get into this private system made him too great a risk, so he had to be eliminated.

Apparently Williams failed to cover his tracks well and got caught, creating a public relations nightmare for MI6. How well does such activity work as a motive for murder?

Since Williams' specific work at MI6 remains, logically, closely guarded from the public, any connection between his death and his position must be speculative. Wilcox admits no evidence in the case points toward MI6 as the culprit.

Although the weather turned warm during the period, the heat in the apartment remained on during the time Williams' body lay in the bag, increasing the speed of decomposition, thereby making the cause of death more difficult to determine. Conspiracy theorists contend this warm climate was intentional for this very purpose.

Russians

Boris Karpichkov, a Russian defector to the U.K., told reporters in fall of 2015 that he knew who had killed Williams: Russian spies. Karphichokov claimed the Russians attempted to lure Williams to work as a double agent. However, his story goes that Williams turned the tables, telling the contact that he knew who must have given the Russians inside information about him, a revelation that Karpichkov says led to the Britain's death since it revealed Williams knew the identity of the Russian agent.

To lend further credibility to his tale, Karpichkov detailed the manner of death, saying the killer placed an untraceable poison into Williams' ear. The published story does not explain how the murderer managed to do so nor why the body was then stuffed into the duffle bag. Although the story seems not to have gained credible support from police, newspapers circulated Karpichkov's tale. It gains some backing because of reports that someone noted Russian Embassy vehicles near Williams' building in the days leading up to finding the body.

Accidental Death

In 2015, Metropolitan police announced their belief that Williams died accidentally, putting himself into the bag and unable to get out. One of the pathologists involved in the case told Wilcox that a person inside such a bag could easily suffocate in minutes. The medical experts agreed suffocation one of the most likely causes of death in the case. After just a couple of minutes, the carbon dioxide levels would rise to the point that the person would encounter difficulty staying awake and focused. They also allowed that moving his arms inside the bag in an attempt to escape would account for the abrasions on the elbows.

Why would anyone lock himself inside a bag? Perhaps to practice escaping if ever in such an emergency? If so, certainly Williams did not know how quickly the carbon monoxide could overtake him. A former landlady told reporters a story about how Williams once needed help in the wee hours of the morning to release him from his bed where he had supposedly tied himself in order to attempt practicing extrication. But this story remains anomalous.

FINAL THOUGHTS

Like so many of the cases here, the contradictory nature of the evidence makes this death puzzling. Experts again and again claimed Williams putting himself inside the bag an impossibility, but then viewers were able to witness such an event in action (see a video of it here: http://www.dailymail.co.uk/video/news/video-10096/Yoga-expert-demonstrates-climb-holdall-inquest.html). So was Williams murdered after all?

Perhaps he was truly a person who enjoyed (or felt it an important aspect of his job) putting himself in difficult situations and finding a way out. Nobody doubts his grand physical shape, and if he had performed such amazing feats before, perhaps he felt himself somewhat invincible. While accidental death in such a manner seems ridiculous on its face, closer examination of the possibility gives the theory legs.

The controversy partly rages because of the lack of a clear motive for murder. Although not as innocent as Julia Wallace, Williams seemed to not move in particularly dangerous circles, even given his position with MI6. Although movies romanticize such jobs, the daily grind of understand hackers, finding their methods and ways to stop them and breaking other codes does not tend to put one in the face of life-threatening peril.

The fact that some of Williams' family members believe a conspiracy afoot does not actually lend support to the murder theory. How often do we hear of loved ones refusing to believe a person was suicidal, could have moonlighted as a serial killer or might have done something so stupid as to lead to his or her death?

However, Williams certainly demonstrated his willingness to compromise his position by giving out confidential information. Perhaps he told one of them something of his concerns, giving their suspicion more credibility. If that were the case, one might think them close enough to have realized he had gone missing sooner and to have raised the alarm rather than waiting for coworkers to notice.

Could any of these spy agencies truly been instrumental in Williams' death? Certainly. They make a business of finding out secrets and making sure their own stay safe. And they have years of practice at covering their tracks when they do commit murder. It just seems the less likely of the two possibilities.

So in the end, the most likely scenario, as unlikely as it might at first seem, appears to be Williams putting himself inside the bag with the expectation of getting himself out, unfortunately forgetting to include a safety net. Why, then, include this case in this tome? One simple question: how did he manage to get in without leaving footprints or palm prints anywhere on the tub or fingerprints on the padlock? Until we see a video demonstrating that, this case will remain an unsolved murder.

Chapter 7: The Sodder Children, Fayetteville, West Virginia

December, 1945

THE DISCOVERY

Christmas Eve, 1945, George and Jennie Sodder spent a fun-filled evening with nine of their ten children opening presents, the celebratory mood hampered only by the fact that one son could not attend since he had joined the military. The household turned in late that evening only to have the silence broken by the shrill of the telephone just after midnight. Jennie rushed to answer it but found the caller had dialed the wrong number. As she quietly returned to bed, she noted one child sleeping on the couch alone with the curtains open and all the downstairs lights ablaze; she assumed the others had all gone to their rooms.

After drawing the curtains, shutting off the lights and locking the front door, Jennie crept back to bed, settling in for a few hours' rest before the chaos of Christmas morning. Just as she began to drift back to sleep, a thump and clang from the roof startled her awake even though the master bedroom was on the ground floor of the house. "Somebody threw something on our roof," she thought to herself. She looked out to determine what had happened but saw nothing untoward in the darkness and so returned once again to her bed, finally slipping into a deep sleep.

Around one o'clock in the morning, Jennie awoke to smoke curling under the bedroom door. Screaming for her husband, she ran to the hallway, anxious to get the family to safety. George jumped up and joined her in hollering for the children asleep upstairs. After grabbing the infant whose crib shared their bedroom, the parents ran outside and counted heads. To their horror, they quickly realized half their children were still inside the burning structure.

Although 17-year-old Marion, who had fallen asleep on the couch, and the two oldest boys still at home – John, 23, and George Jr., 16 – who shared a room upstairs escaped singed but alive from the flames, five children were seemingly trapped in what quickly became an inferno: Maurice, 14; Martha, 12; Louis, 9; Jennie, 8; and Betty, 5.

Frantic to reach the children he imagined trapped in the two second floor bedrooms they shared, George Sr. smashed a window in his attempt to get back inside, cutting himself badly in the process. Flames reached through the window along with choking smoke, making entry there impossible. George ran to the side of the house where he kept a ladder, thinking to climb up to the children, but the trusty tool had vanished.

Inspiration struck, and he hurried to the trucks kept on the property that George used in his coal-hauling business, planning to climb atop one and get to the second story. Although he had run both just the previous day, they refused to start at this crucial time. A barrel sat nearby to collect rainwater, and George struggled to scoop from it to douse the flames. However, the icy weather had frozen the material, making it useless.

As George struggled to get back inside through the raging flames, Marion ran to a neighbor for help but failed to raise the operator from the phone. At the same time, another neighbor spotted the fire and attempted to call officials from a nearby bar with the same effect. Giving up on the phones, the neighbor physically drove to find the fire chief, F.J. Morris, who started the alarm. Just 45 minutes after Jennie awoke, the Sodders' house was gone.

By the time firefighters finally arrived at 8 am Christmas morning, the house had burned completely away along with the lives of five precious youngsters.

THE SCENE

As Christmas dawned that bleak day in 1945, the surviving Sodders stared at all that remained of their home and the youngest children: a basement foundation filled with ashes. The state police inspector and Morris sifted through the remnants, looking for the children's remains. Although apparently the initial search uncovered a few bones, nobody told the family about them. The fire marshal told the Sodders to leave the site so investigators could more thoroughly search after the holidays, and the parents were given no remains to put their children to rest.

George could not leave his children in that manner, however, and so ran a bulldozer over the site of the house before the new year. The survivors planted flowers as a memorial to the children and siblings lost in the fire.

Despite the official ruling that faulty wiring was the cause, evidence mounted at the house that someone had deliberately set the Sodder house on fire. The baby found a hard rubber piece of something in the area, what George decided was the remnants of a pineapple bomb, an explosive device like a hand grenade that explodes on impact and could easily have been what Jennie heard clattering on the roof; perhaps someone threw it to set the house ablaze. A telephone repairman who visited the site said someone had cut the phone lines leading to the house, and a nearby neighbor told George he had seen someone taking a block and tackle, used to remove engines from cars, from the homestead. If the coal truck had no engine, that would certainly account for the truck's failure to start.

As the Sodders attempted to heal their broken family, suspicion regarding the true fate of the children began to grow. Fueled by the belief that officials recovered no bones from the site, rumors flew that someone had kidnapped the five children and set the fire to cover up the crime.

Sightings came in not only from nearby towns, St. Louis, Charleston and as far away as Manhattan. George followed every lead, badgering parents to let him see the children he thought might be his, hiring a private detective who failed to help, contacting the FBI and eventually erecting a billboard at the home site with pictures of the missing children, information about the fire and an offer of a $5000 reward.

Four years after that terrible Christmas, the Sodders hired a pathologist from Washington D.C. to examine the site, who discovered some vertebrae in the ashes. The Smithsonian Institution examined the remains and reported them to seemingly belong to a body of a male several years older than the eldest child thought to perish in the fire. They admitted such a stretch in age was possible, but the lack of evidence of having been through a fire made the bones less credible to belong to any of the Sodders. They announced that a fire of such duration should have left quite a bit of skeletal remains, feeding the Sodders' search for children they increasingly believed had been kidnapped before the fire was set.

No legitimate trace of any of the children was ever found even though neither parent gave up hope. Sadly, George died in 1969 and Jennie two decades after him, neither learning any more about what happened that horrible holiday evening.

THE SUSPECTS

Random Killer or Kidnapper

Afterward, several suspicious incidents came back to George, times people had acted strangely before the fire.

One day that fall, an unknown man had appeared at the house looking for work. George told him he had no need for a laborer, but the man wandered the property for a few minutes, finally pointing out the fuse boxes at the house's rear entrance and stating, "That's going to cause a fire someday." George thought the man's pronouncement odd since he had no concern about the wiring; the power company had just recently inspected the house and declared the wiring fine.

The other incident that stuck out to George involved an insurance salesman who insisted Sodder purchase a policy to protect his home and family. Losing his temper when Sodder refused, the salesman told George that he was going to lose everything, children included, in a fire one day. "Your goddamn house is going up in smoke," George remembered the man shouting. The salesman followed up with a comment about Sodder getting payback for nasty comments about Mussolini. At the time, Sodder felt the remark just a frustrated comment, even with the political barb, but in hindsight, it looked more like a threat. While many in the close-knit Italian community supported Mussolini, Sodder had made no secret of his distaste for the dictator. Had his political leanings led someone to attack his family, killing or kidnapping his children?

George was not the only Sodder examining the months leading up to the fire for clues. The two sons who had home that night recalled a stranger parked along the highway next to the house just before the holiday break, a man who watched the younger Sodder siblings as they returned home at the end of the school day.

No clues led anywhere in this regard. Since officials refused to investigate, claiming the children dead, the fire accidental and the case closed, the Sodders were left on their own to pursue such leads, virtually assuring that no such random arsonist kidnapper would face justice.

The Mafia

After Jennie's death in 1989, her remaining children and their children worked to continue the legacy, investigating on their own to try to solve the mystery. One suggestion they came upon was that the mafia had burned down the house.

The thinking behind this theory involved the local mafia attempting to recruit George into their ranks or that they had aimed to squeeze money from the comfortable Italian-American. Either way, their advances refused, they decided to teach Sodder a lesson by burning down his house with everyone in it.

This kind of conspiracy theory gains traction when looking at the timeline regarding the response to the calls about the fire that night. How could it possibly take seven hours for help to arrive?

The answer to that question lies in the primitive alarm methods at the time. No localized fire siren existed. Instead, one member of the fire team would receive a call, and he in turn would call the next man on the list and so on. Such a method would definitely account for some delay in the response, although an interval of hours and hours seems a bit extreme. Perhaps word got round that the place had burned to the ground in less than an hour, causing the firefighters to feel less compelled to rush to the site. At any rate, the apparently nonchalance of the team together with the attitude of the fire marshal contribute to this rumor's credibility.

Again, the lack of official involvement in an investigation after the fact means this theory will likely never be proven or disproven.

FINAL THOUGHTS

So were the children kidnapped or killed in the fire? The lack of remains found at the site creates the most doubt about their deaths. Dr. William Maples, forensic anthropologist extraordinaire, explains that bones often survive burning in such situations. Crematoriums typically run at about 1700 degrees Fahrenheit in order to reduce most of the bones to ash. A house fire would typically need to burn for a good two hours to reach such temperatures, indicating that it seems some bones should have survived the inferno.

Unfortunately, the Sodders' actions at the time might have prevented a clear resolution to this harrowing story, at least regarding the children's fates. The Smithsonian investigators in the 1940s suggested that any remains could likely have been part of the soil George used to fill in the basement and plant the flower garden memorial, forever lost to forensic study.

A 2005 National Public Radio story interviewed the West Virginia State Fire Marshal, Sterling Lewis, who verified the actions young children typically take in a fire: they hide. Lewis said, "We find them under beds. We find them in closets. We find them crawled up in the bathtubs." The missing children, aged 5 to 14, might well have reacted in such a manner when they awoke to the horror of finding themselves trapped on the second floor.

Had they been kidnapped, what are the chances that none of the five would manage to contact their family at home at some point during the ensuing years? One might believe one or two children, particularly very young ones, might be persuaded their parents were dead or be frightened into subduing. The likelihood of all five, two of them teenagers, never finding a way to get back in touch seems like ridiculous odds.

Even if the mystery of what happened to the children gets put to rest and readers agree the children died in the house fire, who might have set it and why? Was the "wrong number" Jennie received someone checking to see if the family was home? The insurance salesman who threatened George sat on the panel that declared the fire accidental; was this a cover-up?

Apparently, George's political leanings made him something of a target in the community. It does seem possible that an arsonist set the fire as payback for George's beliefs, not caring about the loss of the children's lives. Setting a fire in the middle of the night would typically create the greatest destruction even if everyone inside managed to escape.

As for who might have wanted to destroy the Sodders, each theory seems just as plausible as the next in retrospect. While people today may scoff at the idea of a mafia hit, times were different in the 1940s, particularly in the heat of early World War I. The nationalistic feelings it provoked could well have sparked a fatal fury in someone from the city.

Just as logical, however, remains the possibility of a purely accidental fire. Although the officials seem to have rather hastily reached their conclusion and refused to entertain the possibility of arson, that does not mean they were automatically wrong. Jennie later stated she felt the cause could not have been due to electrical issues since she saw the lights all on when she answered the phone at 12:30. But she also did not see or smell smoke at that time, so the fire likely had not started, at least not in earnest.

Many homes built prior to 1950 used aluminum wiring covered in cloth: haven for a fire to not only start but spread quickly inside the walls. A faulty wire would send a spark, igniting the flammable material and resulting in a fast blaze. The fact that the entire home burned to ash in less than an hour may even support this accidental theory more powerfully. The U.S. Fire Administration indicates that electrical problems caused more than six percent of the house fires in 2013, when buildings use much safer wiring systems.

In the end, they mystery will never be solved. A 2012 interview with the last survivor from the tragedy – the then two-year old Sylvia grown to a 69-year-old woman – emphasizes the true horror of the event. Instead of happy family gatherings and joyful outings, her earliest memories involved the fear and uncertainty of a terrible Christmas morning in 1945 when her family's lives changed forever.

Chapter 8: Janett Christman, Columbia, Missouri

March, 1950

Saturday night, March 18, 1950, Mrs. Romack asked Janett Christman, aged 13, to babysit her three-year-old son. Although the night blew in cold and blustery and the high school Janett attended was throwing a dance, the teenager agreed to sit for Mrs. Romack's toddler. She required the money to purchase a new outfit she had already picked out for Easter. Like most young teenage girls of the era, babysitting represented the only way for her to get the cash she needed.

Janett left the home she shared with her parents above the restaurant they ran and braved the freezing temperatures to reach the Romack's house just outside the city limits of Columbia, Missouri. Ed Romack and his wife planned to attend a party at 8 pm that evening. Neither worried too much at the time that Janett would encounter trouble, but Ed showed the teenager how to use his shotgun kept by the front door just in case. He warned her to turn on the porch light if the doorbell rang, Mrs. Romack assured her the toddler would likely sleep well with the radio on, and the couple hurried off to their evening away.

At 10:35, the phone rang at the local police station. Officer Roy McGowan picked up the receiver and was greeted by hysterical screaming on the other end. The only words he was able to make out were "Come quick" before the girl dropped the phone. Unable to trace the call, the officer helplessly listened in vain for more information about who was calling and where she was before the line went dead.

The storm picked up at about 11 pm, and Mrs. Romack called her house to check on Janett, worried the lightning might have awakened her son. However, she got a busy signal. Having a party line (a single line shared by multiple households), she did not fret about being unable to reach the teenager and returned to the party.

Janett's friend Carol Haley Holt, also babysitting that stormy night, said she felt uncomfortable that evening, an unease that grew about midnight. Her disquiet increased so much that she double-checked the front door to assure herself it was locked tight, and she looked in on her charge, who was sleeping peacefully.

The Romacks left the party shortly before 1:30 am and headed home. Instead of finding the house as they had left it, they discovered disturbing signs: the back door sat wide open, and the front door was closed but unlocked. Ed Romack entered cautiously only to find Janett's body on the living room floor.

THE SCENE

Bloody fingerprints, handprints and splashes adorned not only the living room but the kitchen where the phone hung from the wall and the hallway between the two rooms, decorating the walls and floor in horrifying red. The killer had cut an electrical cord from the Romacks' iron and wrapped it around Janett's neck. Her bloody head indicated a beating, as well, and the position of her body and clothing pointed to some kind of sexual assault. Bloody scratches marred her young face. The pathologist who examined the body, Dr. M.P. Neal, determined the murderer struck the teen with a small blunt, metallic object, leaving punctures in her skull, but officials found no such weapon on the scene. Although the blows were forceful, Neal concluded Janett died from asphyxiation due to strangulation with the cord and had indeed been raped. He announced death occurred between 10:30 and 11:30 that evening, but the frantic phone call placed the time closer to the former.

A window on the side of the house had been smashed from the outside, creating what the police assumed the attacker used to gain entry to the house. However, a piano sat directly in front of the broken pane on which sat numerous undisturbed trinkets.

This Is House Where Baby Sitter Was Slain

Police quickly called in tracking dogs that followed a scent from the house to a nearby corner, where they lost the trail, leaving little evidence usable in those days to find the killer. Officials questioned dozens of men in the days and weeks after Janett's murder but found little to support an arrest. They were left with the increasing suspicion that Janett's killer knew his way around the Romack's house, a collection of bloody fingerprints and little else.

THE SUSPECT

Robert Mueller

Although police looked in several directions in the case, only one man truly stood out as a suspect: Robert Mueller. Looking back, it is unclear exactly why Mueller first appeared on police radar, but the lead investigator, Sheriff Glen Powell, soon zeroed in on the young man.

Regardless of how he initially became a suspect, Mueller, aged 27, looked good for the killing for a variety of reasons. First, he knew the Romack house well. A friend of Ed's, Mueller had spent time at the home, visiting on more than one occasion before the attack.

He also knew Janett. Witnesses at a later hearing testified Mueller commented multiple times on Janett's virginity and "well-developed figure," which he admired. He had called Janett to ask her to sit for a youngster at his house that Saturday night only to be told Janett had already promised the Romacks. So Mueller not only had commented rudely about Janett but was aware she would be alone at the Romacks' house that night.

Whether due to the police interest or some other reason, some of Mueller's friends and acquaintances apparently also thought him capable of Janett's murder. Romack testified that Mueller told him once, "I might have done it and then forgotten it." Ed Romack might have been persuaded to turn against his friend after discussing the case with his wife. She told her husband that she felt uncomfortable around Mueller and further confessed to the grand jury that Mueller had touched her inappropriately just days before her date to give evidence. Clearly, Mueller felt unconcerned about the potential charges facing him and cared little about boundaries of appropriate behavior with women.

Then there is the matter of the weapon. Mueller habitually carried with him a mechanical pencil. That is, a small metal, blunt object. And the size and shape of the tool seemingly matched the wounds on Janett's body.

The case was far from closed, however. Brought in for extensive questioning about six weeks after the murders, Mueller took a lie-detector test – and passed. At that time, law enforcement, legal officials and the general public put much more stock into such techniques, and a grand jury refused to indict Mueller for Jannet's murder.

FINAL THOUGHTS

The Christman case was just the latest in a string of sexual assaults in the area. Numerous young woman reported attacks, many within their own homes or while babysitting. One case ended in the death of another young woman just a couple blocks away from the Romacks' house: Marylou Jenkins.

Marylou's death occurred four years prior to the attack on Janett Christman, but the similarities between the cases are striking besides the proximity of the houses. Marylou, only 20 years old, had spent the night alone since her mother was nursing next door neighbors. No sign of a break-in was evident, and Marylou's mother had to climb through a window the next morning to gain entry to the house, where she found her lifeless daughter. A cord that had been cut from a lamp wrapped around Marylou's throat, and the young woman had been raped. She struggled violently against her assailant, ripping off many of her fingernails in during the assault, but to no avail. The attack likely occurred about 10 pm since some people in the neighborhood heard screams at that time, even through the incredible storm that hit the city. Unfortunately, none of the people who noticed the screams heeded them and investigated the ruckus.

Clearly, Marylou Jenkins and Janett Christman met the same killer. Could that killer have been Robert Mueller? Not according to official records, since a man was arrested for the murder just a month later. Floyd Cochran, an African-American man with a low IQ, collected trash at the Jenkins house and so had seen Marylou. After initially confessing to the crime, he recanted just before his execution in 1947, two and a half years before Janett met her grisly death.

False confessions certainly do occur, even today, and for an African-American in racially charged Columbia in the 1940s, police could very well have pressured him into confessing. Cochran undoubtedly killed his wife in a domestic squabble, so he was capable of murder. But the question is, did he really kill Marylou Jenkins? The coincidental connections between the murders of Marylou and Janett just cannot be ignored, making it apparent that Cochran was actually not guilty of Jenkins' death.

Some evidence does point to Mueller as a suspect in the attack on Marylou Jenkins, as well. The two of them knew each other, which would account for the lack of indication of a break-in; she might have let him in. He lived near both the Jenkins and Romack houses, all within several blocks of each other. Together with the MO, particularly the strangulation with a cord cut from an appliance in the home, along with the other similarities suggests Mueller might have been guilty of both attacks.

One single bit of the scene at the Romacks' house stands out as implicating Mueller or someone very like him in Janett's murder: the broken window. As mentioned, police assumed the killer gained entry there and fled through the back door, accounting for it being open when the homeowners returned. Some accounts say the blind for the window was open when police arrived, but pictures taken at the scene show it closed and none of the items on top of the piano disturbed. How then could an intruder have entered there? Anyone who has moved a slatted blind to look out or dust knows they are notoriously difficult to keep straight when disturbed.

So why would the attacker break the window at all? The answer may lie in the shotgun Ed Romack so famously kept by the front door. Someone familiar with Romack and his home would likely know about the gun. If that same someone wanted to break in and attack a young girl alone there, he would need to distract the girl from the front door, perhaps getting her to run to the back where the phone was to call for help. Janett managed to make that call.

It seems the proof or exoneration of Mueller should have been easy at the time and easier still now since the Christman scene in particular yielded numerous fingerprints. If they matched Mueller, he could not claim they came from an earlier visit since the prints were caked in Janett's blood. Why did officials at the time make no mention of the connection or lack thereof?

In 2013, reporter Bill Clark determined to uncover the truth by examining the old records. To his chagrin, he discovered that not only the fingerprint evidence from the case but none of the records of physical evidence could be found. It had all disappeared, and with it, the chance of ever determining for certain who killed Janett Christman and, very likely, Marylou Jenkins.

Although Janett was laid to rest on what would have been her 14th birthday, Columbia was never the same. Babysitters became impossible to find as fear took hold of the populace. And the friends of Janett Christman struggled to deal with the horror of losing their friend.

Note:

Information within this text has been verified by using multiple sources including police files whenever possible.

Sources

Abbott, Karen. "The Children Who Went up in Smoke." Smithsonian.com.

"Alice May Hill Burnham." Findagrave.com.

Archive.org. A repository of free information and photos.

Asher, Dean, Sarah Cox and Nancy Stiles. "A History of Violence: Mary Lou Jenkins." *Vox: from The Missourian.* May 12, 2011.

BBC News. "Body of MI6 worker Gareth Williams 'locked in bag'." Sept. 1, 2010.

Cavendish, Marshall. *Murder Casebook (Vol. 71): Ritual Killings.* 1991.

Chandler, Raymond. *Raymond Chandler Speaking.* U. of California Press, 1997.

The Chicago Tribune. March, 1950.

Clark, Bill. "Unsolved murder brought back to spotlight." *Columbia Daily Tribune.* August 19, 2013.

Colorado Springs Gazette. September 21, 22 & 28, 1911. Colorado Springs, CO.

Cutler, Robert. *The Mysterious Death of Jane Stanford.* Stanford U. Press, 2003.

Davies, Caroline. "Gareth Williams probably died by suffocation or poisoning, inquest told." *The Guardian.* April 30, 2012.

Davies, Caroline, James Meikle and agencies. "Gareth Williams's death was 'criminally mediated', says coroner." *The Guardian.* May 2, 2012.

Eleftheriou-Smith, Loulla-Mae. "MI6 spy Gareth Williams was 'killed by Russia for refusing to become double agent', former KGB man claims. *The Independent.* Sept. 8, 2015.

The Electrical Connection. "House Rewires." http://www.theelectricconnection.com/services/house-rewire/

Emery, Erin. "Hot on the trail of cold 1911 ax murders." *The Denver Post*. April 9, 2007.

Everest University Online. "A Quick History of Fingerprinting." Everestonline.edu.

Fabian, Robert. *Anatomy of Crime*. Pelham Publishers. 1970.

Greaney, T.J. "Who Killed Janett Christman?" *Columbia Daily Tribune*. January 22, 2013.

Horn, Stacy. "Mystery of Missing Children Haunts. W.Va. Town." NPR. December 23, 2005.

Jeavons, Ron. "Witchcraft Murder in Long Compton." http://www.rootsweb.ancestry.com/~engcbanb/families/jeavons/jeavons01.htm.

Jesse, F. Tennyson. "Checkmate." 1953.

Johnson, George C. "Strychnine." Southern Illinois University. 1999.

Maples, William R. *Dead Men Do Tell Tales*. Doubleday, 1994.

The New York Times. March, 1905.

Pengelly, Adrian. "Charles Watson – 50 Years On." 1995. http://www.whitedragon.org.uk/articles/charles.htm.

"Slays Six Persons in Near-by Houses." *The New York Times*. September 21, 1911.

Stanton, Jenny. "Spy found dead in a bag 'had infuriated his MI6 bosses by illegally hacking into secret US data on Bill Clinton'." *The Daily Mail*. August 30, 2015.

U.S. Fire Administration. "U.S. Fire Statistics." http://www.usfa.fema.gov/data/statistics/

University of Applied Sciences for Administration and Law at Fuerstenfeldbruck. *Der Mordfall Hinterkaifeck (The Murder Case Hinterkaifeck)*. 2007.

Wilkes, Roger. *Wallace: The Final Verdict*. Grafton, 1984.

Wolfe, Susan. "Who Killed Jane Stanford?" *Stanford Magazine*, September/October 2003.

Zeman, Joshua. *Killer Legends*. 2014.

About the Author

K.M. Sweet's career as a writer and educator has spanned over 30 years, teaching writing, communications, humanities and psychology. A Colorado native with three grown children and one granddaughter, she currently lives on the western slope with her husband. Follow her on Facebook!

Cover art by Thunder Mountain Photography

CPSIA information can be obtained at www.ICGtesting.com
Printed in the USA
BVOW06s0757180916

462487BV00039B/526/P